OFFICIALLY
WITHDRAWN

LIGHTNING BOLT BOOKS™

Golden Retrievers

Sarah Frank

Lerner Publications • Minneapolis

Lerner Publications Company
A division of Lerner Publishing Group, Inc.
241 First Avenue North
Minneapolis, MN 55401 USA

For reading level and more information, look up this title at www.lernerbooks.com.

Library of Congress Cataloging-in-Publication Data

Names: Frank, Sarah, author.
Title: Golden retrievers / Sarah Frank.
Description: Minneapolis : Lerner Publications, [2019] | Series: Lightning bolt books. Who's a good dog? | Audience: Age 6-9. | Audience: Grade K to 3. | Includes bibliographical references and index.
Identifiers: LCCN 2018004398 | ISBN 9781541538603 (lb : alk. paper)
Subjects: LCSH: Golden retriever—Juvenile literature.
Classification: LCC SF429.G63 F73 2019 | DDC 636.752/7—dc23

LC record available at https://lccn.loc.gov/2018004398

Manufactured in the United States of America
1-45043-35870-6/13/2018

Table of Contents

They Are Golden!

Meet a special dog. This pooch is friendly. It also loves to have fun! It's a golden retriever.

Goldens have big hearts to match their big bodies.

Golden retrievers are often called goldens for short. They are big bundles of love. They weigh from 55 to 75 pounds (25 to 34 kg). They are about 23 inches (58 cm) high.

Goldens have lots of energy. They do well on hikes or runs. Many goldens also enjoy swimming.

Throw a toy into the water, and watch your golden go for it!

Love that golden smile!

Lots of people choose goldens as pets. Some golden owners say their dog's feelings show on its face. Goldens always seem to be smiling!

About Golden Retrievers

Different dogs have different personalities. Dogs also come in different sizes. But some dog breeds have things in common. The American Kennel Club (AKC) groups breeds by things they have in common.

Goldens are in the sporting group. All sporting dogs are active and alert. Many also make great hunting dogs.

Goldens are originally from Scotland. In the nineteenth century, they worked as hunting dogs for the rich. Later, people took these dogs to the United States.

This golden hangs out in Scotland—the original home of goldens.

Goldens are fun, furry family members.

Families in the United States just loved goldens! They still do. It's easy to see why.

The Right Choice?

Not every pet is right for every family. Decide with your family whether a golden is right for you.

Goldens have spunk. They need lots of exercise. Are you too busy to walk a golden every day? Then a cat might be a better pet.

Goldens need room to move around and stretch out. Does your home have plenty of space? If not, pass on a big dog.

Goldens need to spend time with you. If you're in lots of after-school activities, your golden could get lonely. And lonely goldens can cause trouble.

Ruh-roh!

Take Good Care

Do you still want a golden? Then you're in for some fun. But first, you need supplies. Think bowls, a leash, toys, and more.

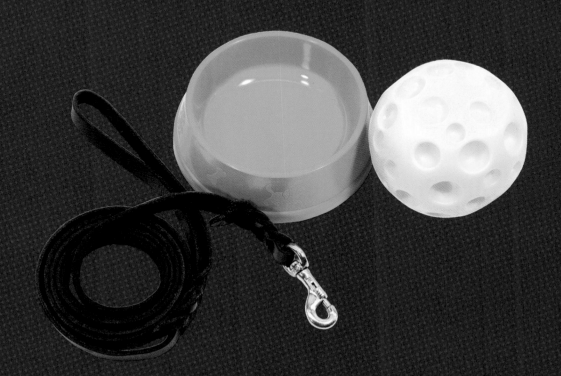

Next, find a vet for your golden. Your dog will need to see the vet right away. The vet will check it for health problems.

Dogs need food and water, so set out some doggy bowls as soon as you bring your golden home. Keep your dog on a dog food diet. Table scraps aren't good for dogs.

A vet can help you choose a good dog food.

Aw, puppy love!

You're on your way to being a great golden owner. Be there for your dog. Your pooch needs you even when you're busy or tired. You'll be rewarded with lots of golden kisses.

Doggone Good Tips!

- Your dog should have a super name. Here are some great names for goldens: Goldie, Sunny, Sandy, Dazzler, or Lyric.

- Not sure you're up for training a new puppy? See if your local humane society has an adult golden you could adopt. Adult goldens are usually trained already.

- Get a good vacuum if you get a golden! These dogs shed—a lot. But their owners say the mess is more than worth it.

Why Goldens Are the Best

- Their fur is special! They have a double coat. This means they have two layers of fur. The layers keep them warm in the winter. And water won't stick to a golden's fur. They can play outside on a rainy day and be dry before you know it.

- Some goldens work as guide dogs for the blind. They can also be trained to help a person in a wheelchair. These working goldens are true heroes.

- Well-trained goldens usually get along with every member of the family—even cats!

Glossary

alert: watchful and quick to act

American Kennel Club (AKC): an organization that groups dogs by breed

breed: a particular type of dog. Dogs of the same breed have the same body shape and general features.

diet: the food that a person or an animal eats every day

personality: the behavior or qualities that make one person or animal different from others

sporting group: a group of dogs that are active, alert, and known for performing well outdoors and in the water

spunk: spirit or liveliness

vet: a doctor who treats animals

Further Reading

American Kennel Club
http://www.akc.org

American Society for the Prevention of Cruelty to
Animals
https://www.aspca.org

Boothroyd, Jennifer. *Hero Service Dogs.* Minneapolis:
Lerner Publications, 2017.

Gray, Susan H. *Golden Retrievers.* New York: AV2 by
Weigl, 2018.

Statts, Leo. *Golden Retrievers*. Minneapolis: Abdo
Zoom, 2017.

Index

Photo Acknowledgments

Image credits: Diego Lezama/Lonely Planet Images/Getty Images, p. 2; MirasWonderland/
Shutterstock.com, pp. 4, 23; In Green/Shutterstock.com, p. 5; everydoghasastory/
Shutterstock.com, p. 6; Petra Wegner/Nature Picture Library/Getty Images, p. 7; cynoclub/
Shutterstock.com, p. 8; mariannehoy/iStock/Getty Images, p. 9; Image copyright
of S Turner/Moment/Getty Images, p. 10; Paul Barton/Corbis/Getty Images, p. 11;
wavebreakmedia/Shutterstock.com, p. 12; Monkey Business Images/Shutterstock.com, p. 13;
K.Phaitoon Bualaor/Shutterstock.com, p. 14; Jeroen van den Broek/Shutterstock.com, p. 15;
Bulltus_casso/Shutterstock.com, p. 16; romul014/Shutterstock.com, p. 17; Elena Elisseeva/
Shutterstock.com, p. 18; Ted Horowitz/Corbis/Getty Images, p. 19.

Cover: GlobalP/iStock/Getty Images.

Main body text set in Billy Infant regular 28/36. Typeface provided by SparkType.